W9-ABT-389

5741567

c)

J
919
.69
Rus

Russell, William, 1942-
  Hawaii / William Russell. -- Vero Beach : Rourke
Book Co., c1994.
  24 p. : ill., map. -- (Islands in the sea)

Includes index.
0772828X   LC:93049340   ISBN:1559160349 (lib. bdg.)

1. Hawaii - Description and travel. I. Title

PICKERING PUBLIC LIBRARY
CENTRAL BRANCH

260235   95JAN23   32/06 3-01040167

HAWAII

ISLANDS IN THE SEA

William Russell

The Rourke Book Co., Inc.
Vero Beach, Florida 32964

© 1994 The Rourke Book Co., Inc.

All rights reserved. No part of this book may be reproduced or utilized in any form or by any means, electronic or mechanical including photocopying, recording or by any information storage and retrieval system without permission in writing from the publisher.

Edited by Sandra A. Robinson

PHOTO CREDITS
© James P. Rowan: cover, pages 7, 12, 13, 15, 18;
courtesy Hawaii Visitors Bureau: title page, pages 4, 8, 10, 17

Library of Congress Cataloging-in-Publication Data

Russell, William, 1942-
    Hawaii / by William Russell.
        p.   cm. — (Islands in the sea)
    Includes index.
    ISBN 1-55916-034-9
    1. Hawaii—Juvenile literature. [1. Hawaii.] I. Title. II. Series.
DU623.25.R87   1994
919.69—dc20   93-49340
                                                      CIP
                                                      AC

TABLE OF CONTENTS

HAWAII

Hawaii is America's only island state. It is the only one of the 50 United States that is not part of North America. Even though it is 2,500 miles away from North America, Hawaii is a favorite vacation land for Americans.

The chain of 132 Hawaiian Islands spreads across about 1,600 miles of the north central Pacific Ocean. Together, the Hawaiian Islands cover 6,471 square miles. That is about the size of Connecticut and Rhode Island combined.

Kauai is one of 132 islands that make up the state of Hawaii

OAHU AND THE OTHER ISLANDS

Hawaii has eight main islands — Niihau, Kauai, Oahu, Molokai, Lanai, Maui, Kahoolawe and Hawaii. Each island is special.

Oahu is the busiest and most-often visited island. Honolulu, Hawaii's capital and largest city, is there. The world-famous Waikiki Beach is in Honolulu.

The *USS Arizona* Memorial is near Honolulu. Japanese warplanes sank the battleship *Arizona* when they attacked Pearl Harbor on December 7, 1941. The United States decided to fight in World War II after this attack.

World-famous Waikiki Beach is on the Hawaiian island of Oahu

VISITING HAWAII

Hawaii attracts thousands of tourists all year round. Visitors enjoy **hula** dancing, the music of Hawaiian guitars, and gardens of bright flowers.

Hawaii has a warm, comfortable climate and long, sandy beaches with tall, rolling waves called **breakers.** It also has forests, canyons, mountains and moonlike **lava** fields.

Hawaiians welcome visitors with long wreaths of flowers, called **leis.** They greet visitors by saying "Aloha" — the same word they use to say goodbye!

Thundering winter waves bring surfers to Hawaiian shores

HAWAII'S VOLCANOES

Hawaii is almost as well-known for its **volcanoes** as it is for its ocean beaches. Volcanoes are openings in the Earth's surface. They are caused by heat and pressure building up deep in the Earth. Volcanoes erupt burning rock called lava, gases and other substances.

The creation of the Hawaiian Islands began when undersea volcanoes erupted about 6 million years ago.

Hawaii's two active volcanoes are Mauna Loa and Kilauea. Mauna Kea is a dormant, or "sleeping," volcano. It is no longer active. Mauna Kea is the highest point of land in the Hawaiian Islands.

The volcano Kilauea erupts in Hawaii Volcanoes National Park on the island of Hawaii, the "Big Island"

The nene goose, Hawaii's state bird, nearly became extinct

*Clouds brush Haleakala Crater, the creation of a volcano in
Haleakala National Park on Maui*

HAWAII LONG AGO

Polynesians came by boat to Hawaii from other Pacific islands about 1,600 years ago. They were the first, or **native,** Hawaiians.

Most of the world didn't know about Hawaii until 1778. Then Captain James Cook of the English Navy "discovered" the islands.

The United States made Hawaii a **territory** in 1900. Hawaii became the 50th state in 1959.

The Polynesian Cultural Center on Oahu is a showplace of the old Polynesian way of life

PEOPLE OF HAWAII

People from many backgrounds live in Hawaii. Some are native Polynesians. Far more Hawaiians belong to other groups — Japanese, Chinese, Filipino, and white and black people from the mainland United States. Nearly all Hawaiians speak English.

About four out of every five Hawaiians live on the island of Oahu. Almost everyone else lives on one of six other main islands.

Flowers hide a Hawaiian
miss wearing a head lei

LIVING IN HAWAII

Because they live on small islands, Hawaiians cannot travel long distances by road. They "island hop" — travel from one island to another — by plane or boat.

Hawaii has few natural resources — like minerals — or factories. Most products that Hawaiians use are imported.

Very little of Hawaii can be farmed. However, the islands produce large crops of pineapples and sugar cane.

Volcanic rock, mountains and canyons, like Waimea on Kauai, make farming difficult in Hawaii

HAWAII'S WONDERS

Hawaii's beauty is often breathtaking. Its two national parks — Haleakala on Maui and Hawaii Volcanoes on the island of Hawaii — are filled with wonders. Visitors to Hawaii Volcanoes National Park can sometimes see the volcanoes Manua Loa and Kilauea erupt with smoke and fire.

Another wonder is Mount Waialeale on Kauai. Mount Waialeale is the wettest place in the world that is not underwater. Waialeale usually gets more than one inch of rain every day!

THE HAWAIIAN ISLANDS

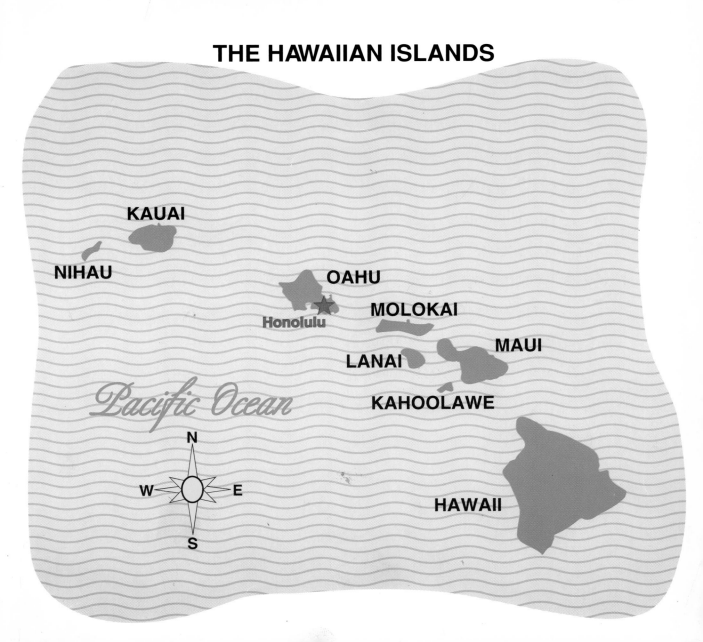

HAWAII'S WILDLIFE

Almost all the wild Hawaiian animals and plants are found nowhere else on Earth.

Most Hawaiian wildlife is either a bird, an insect or a snail. The islands have only two kinds of native mammals — seals and bats.

Animals brought to the Hawaiian Islands by settlers have destroyed native animals. Mongooses, for example, have killed thousands of birds.

Many kinds of Hawaiian birds are **extinct** — they are gone forever. Many others are in danger of becoming extinct.

Glossary

breakers (BRAY kerz) — tall, rolling waves

extinct (ex TINKT) — no longer existing

hula (HOO la) — a type of Polynesian dance in which the dancers' hands and hips move in rhythm

lava (LAH vuh) — melted rock that pours out of a volcano and later hardens

lei (LAY) — a Hawaiian wreath of flowers or leaves

native (NAY tihv) — referring to people, plants or animals that are *found naturally* in an area, and not people, plants or animals that are *brought into* an area

territory (TARE rih tor ee) — a part of the United States, but not a state

volcano (vahl KAY no) — an opening in the Earth caused by underground forces, and the mountain of rock that forms around it

INDEX

PICKERING PUBLIC LIBRARY